I Go To School

By Latifah Jones

Scott Foresman
is an imprint of

Glenview, Illinois • Boston, Massachusetts • Chandler, Arizona •
Upper Saddle River, New Jersey

I ride a bus.

I ride a boat.

I ride a horse.

I ride in a car.

I ride a train.

I ride a bike.

I run.